Favourite Nursery Rhymes

Illustrated by Mandy Stanley

HarperCollins *Children's Books*

Jack and Jill

Jack and Jill went up the hill

To fetch a pail of water.

Jack fell down and broke his crown,

And Jill came tumbling after!

Little Bo-Peep

Little Bo-Peep has lost her sheep,

And doesn't know where to find them;

Leave them alone, and they'll come home,

Bringing their tails behind them.

Humpty Dumpty

Humpty Dumpty sat on a wall,

Humpty Dumpty had a great fall.

All the king's horses and all the king's men

Couldn't put Humpty together again.

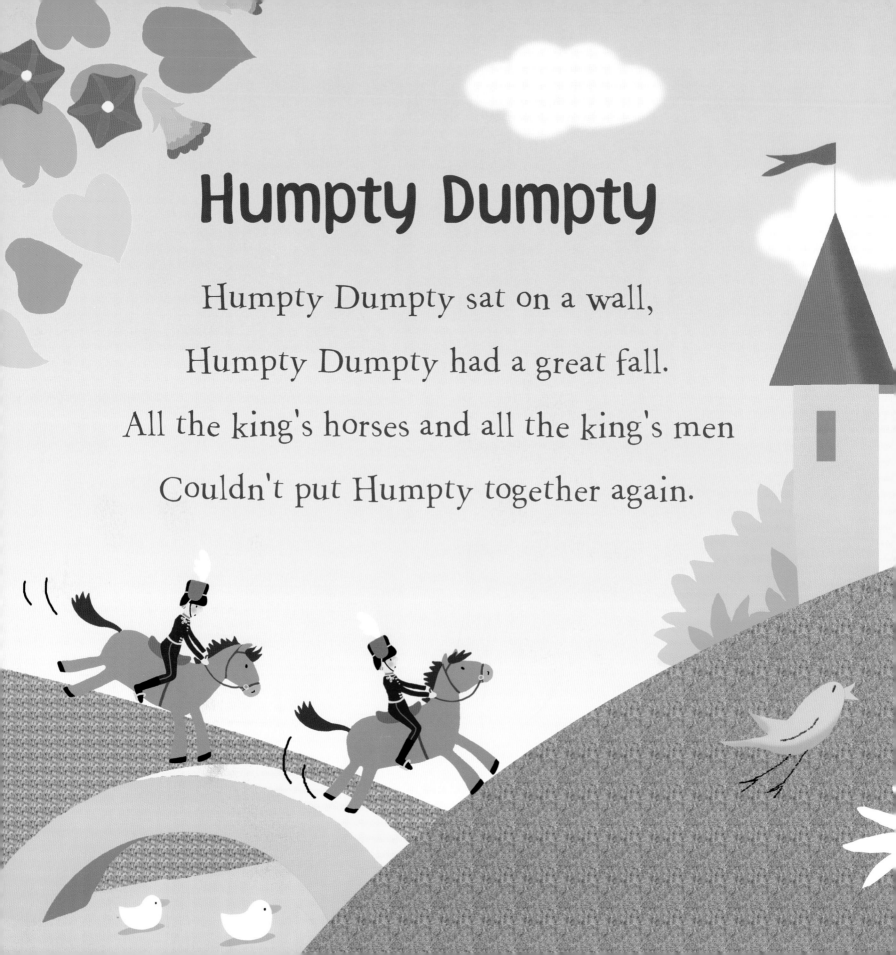

Mary, Mary, Quite Contrary

Mary, Mary, quite contrary,

How does your garden grow?

With silver bells and cockle shells,

And pretty maids all in a row.

Little Boy Blue

Little Boy Blue,

Come blow your horn,

The sheep's in the meadow,

The cow's in the corn.

But where is the boy

Who looks after the sheep?

He's under a haystack

Fast asleep!

Little Miss Muffet

Little Miss Muffet

Sat on a tuffet,

Eating her curds and whey.

Along came a spider,

Who sat down beside her

And frightened Miss Muffet away.

Mary Had a Little Lamb

Mary had a little lamb,

Its fleece was white as snow,

And everywhere that Mary went,

The lamb was sure to go.

Davy Davy Dumpling

Davy Davy Dumpling,

Boil him in the pot;

Sugar him and butter him,

And eat him while he's hot.

Polly Put the Kettle On

Polly put the kettle on,

Polly put the kettle on,

Polly put the kettle on,

We'll all have tea.

This Little Piggy Went to Market

This little piggy went to market,

This little piggy stayed at home,

This little piggy had roast beef,

This little piggy had none,

And this little piggy cried,

"Wee-wee! Wee-wee!",

All the way home.

Wee-wee!
Wee-wee!

The Wheels on the Bus

The wheels on the bus

Go round and round,

Round and round,

Round and round.

The wheels on the bus

Go round and round,

All day long.

Incy Wincy Spider

Incy Wincy spider

Climbed up the water spout.

Down came the rain

And washed the spider out.

Out came the sunshine

And dried up all the rain,

And Incy Wincy spider

Climbed up the spout again.

I'm a Little Teapot

I'm a little teapot, short and stout,

Here's my handle, here's my spout.

When I get all steamed up, hear me shout,

"Tip me up and pour me out!"

Ring-a-Ring o'Roses

Ring-a-ring o'roses,

A pocket full of posies,

A-tishoo! A-tishoo!

We all fall down.

Horsie, Horsie

Horsie, horsie, don't you stop,

Just let your feet go clipetty clop;

Your tail goes swish,

and the wheels go round –

Giddy up, you're homeward bound!

Pat-a-Cake

Pat-a-cake, pat-a-cake, baker's man,

Bake me a cake as fast as you can.

Pat it and prick it and mark it with 'B',

Put it in the oven for Baby and me!

The Grand Old Duke of York

Oh, the grand old Duke of York,

He had ten thousand men;

He marched them up to the top of the hill,

And he marched them down again.

And when they were up, they were up,

And when they were down, they were down,

And when they were only halfway up,

They were neither up nor down.

Round and Round the Garden

Round and round the garden,

Like a teddy bear.

One step, two step,

Tickle you under there!

Row, Row, Row Your Boat

Row, row, row your boat,

Gently down the stream.

Merrily, merrily, merrily, merrily,

Life is but a dream.

Three Little Kittens

Three little kittens
They lost their mittens,
And they began to cry,
"Oh, Mother dear, we sadly fear
Our mittens we have lost."

"What? Lost your mittens,
You naughty kittens!
Then you shall have no pie.
Mee-ow, mee-ow, mee-ow.
No, you shall have no pie."

Hickory, Dickory, Dock

Hickory, dickory, dock,

The mouse ran up the clock.

The clock struck one,

The mouse ran down,

Hickory, dickory, dock.

Over in the Meadow

Over in the meadow,

in the sand, in the sun,

Lived an old mother frog

and her little froggy, one.

"Croak," said the mother.

"I croak," said the one.

So they croaked and they croaked

in the sand, in the sun.

Baa, Baa, Black Sheep

Baa, baa, black sheep,

Have you any wool?

Yes, sir, yes, sir,

Three bags full.

One for the master,

And one for the dame,

And one for the little boy

Who lives down the lane.

One, Two, Three, Four, Five

One, two, three, four, five,

Once I caught a fish alive;

Six, seven, eight, nine, ten,

Then I let it go again.

Why did you let it go?

Because it bit my finger so.

Which finger did it bite?

This little finger on the right.

Five Currant Buns

Five currant buns in a baker's shop,

Big and round with a cherry on the top.

Along came a boy with a penny one day,

Bought a currant bun and took it away.

One Potato, Two Potato

One potato, two potato,

Three potato, four.

Five potato, six potato,

Seven potato, MORE!

Five Little Monkeys

Five little monkeys jumping on the bed,

One fell off and bumped his head.

Mama called the doctor and the doctor said,

"No more monkeys jumping on the bed!"

Sing a Song of Sixpence

Sing a song of sixpence,

A pocket full of rye,

Four and twenty blackbirds

Baked in a pie.

When the pie was opened,

The birds began to sing.

Wasn't that a dainty dish

To set before the King?

Twinkle, Twinkle, Little Star

Twinkle, twinkle, little star,

How I wonder what you are.

Up above the world so high,

Like a diamond in the sky;

Twinkle, twinkle, little star,

How I wonder what you are.

Rock-a-bye, Baby

Rock-a-bye, baby

In the tree top,

When the wind blows,

The cradle will rock.

When the bough breaks,

The cradle will fall,

And down will come baby,

Cradle and all.

Diddle, Diddle, Dumpling

Diddle, diddle, dumpling, my son John,

Went to bed with his trousers on;

One shoe off, and one shoe on,

Diddle, diddle, dumpling, my son John.

Star Light, Star Bright

Star light, star bright,

First star I see tonight,

I wish I may, I wish I might,

Have the wish I wish tonight.

Wee Willie Winkie

Wee Willie Winkie

Runs through the town,

Upstairs and downstairs

In his nightgown,

Rapping at the window,

Crying through the lock,

"Are the children all in bed,

For now it's eight o'clock?"

Hey Diddle, Diddle

Hey diddle, diddle,

The cat and the fiddle,

The cow jumped over the moon.

The little dog laughed to see such fun,

And the dish ran away with the spoon.

Come, Let's to Bed

"Come, let's to bed,"

Says Sleepy-head.

"Tarry a while," says Slow.

"Put on the pot,"

Says Greedy Nan,

"We'll sup before we go."

The Man in the Moon

The Man in the Moon

Looked out of the moon,

Looked out of the moon and said,

"'Tis time for all children on the earth

To think about getting to bed!"

Sleep, Baby, Sleep

Sleep, baby, sleep,

Your father tends the sheep,

Your mother shakes the dreamland tree,

And from it fall sweet dreams for thee,

Sleep, baby, sleep,

Sleep, baby, sleep.

Now the Day is Over

Now the day is over,

Night is drawing nigh,

Shadows of the evening

Steal across the sky.

Now the darkness gathers,

Stars begin to peep,

Birds and beasts and flowers

Soon will be asleep.

Sabine Baring-Gould